Mel Bay Presents

WES MONTGOMERY
THE EARLY YEARS

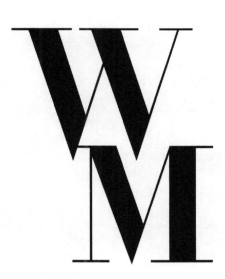

Transcribed by
Dan Bowden

CD CONTENTS

1	Scrambled Eggs [3:20]	6	Tune-Up [4:29]
2	Compulsion [6:48]	7	Says You [5:00]
3	Terrain [7:46]	8	Delirium [3:38]
4	Ursula [7:06]	9	No Hard Feelings [3:47]
5	Lolita [8:06]		

Visit us on the Web at http://www.melbay.com — E-mail us at email@melbay.com

Contents

Wes Montgomery
Photo by Duncan P. Schiedt

Preface

Wes Montgomery
Born in Indianapolis, Indiana March 6, 1925
Died June 15, 1968

Wes Montgomery was a guitarist who developed an incredibly personal style. He was influenced greatly in his early years by the driving single line jazz guitar solos of Charlie Christian. Later, tenor saxophonist John Coltrane had tremendous influence on him. Wes Montgomery possessed a great ear and got one of his first "gigs" playing Charlie Christian solos by ear with a jazz combo. It was later said that his ear was good enough to allow him to remember and embellish any piece, no matter how intricate, after hearing it only once.

Wes Montgomery's style was so unique it can still be recognized by listening to only a measure or two of one of his solos. To begin with, he played with his right hand thumb. The story goes that he developed this technique trying to practice softly so as not to disturb his neighbors. His thumb technique was unbelievably adept, amazing in the words of some observers. This thumb technique gave his playing a warm, gentle timbre. Thus, when listening to Wes, you would hear wonderfully bluesy, "be-bop" phrases laid out in a warm, lyrically intimate manner.

Perhaps the most identifiable aspect of his style, however, was his "funky", virtuosic use of octaves. Many great jazz guitarists have since emulated this stylistic technique but it was pioneered by Wes Montgomery. He proved that rapid and extended solos in octaves could be executed technically and musically. While many others have copied this technique, few seem to obtain Wes' warm, earthy, tone.

Wes' career took a big jump when famed alto saxophonist Cannonball Adderly heard him at an after-hours jazz club in Indianapolis called the Missile Room. A phone call from Adderly set things in motion and not long after, Wes was signed to a record contract with Riverside. He later recorded on the Verve and A & M labels. His was the dominant voice in jazz guitar in the 1960s. His plaudits included winning the *Downbeat*, *Billboard* and *Playboy* jazz guitar polls. He was awarded a Grammy for his solo rendition of the song, "Goin' Out Of My Head." *Time* and *Newsweek* ran stories on him. He played with many if not most of the great jazz sidemen of his era.

We are honored to present this collection of some of Wes Montgomery's early recorded solos from the Riverside collection. We highly recommend the companion cassette. Also available is an additional printed collection of some of his finest recorded solos titled *Wes Montgomery/Jazz Guitar Artistry*.

William Bay

Notes From the Transcriber

This collection of transcribed performances is a sampling from the early recorded work of Wes Montgomery on the Riverside label. Wes signed on with Riverside in the autumn of 1959 and remained with the label through 1963.

These transcriptions capture Wes in contrasting settings and roles; as sideman, leader and with various group configurations. As a sideman, Wes improvised concisely, offering exactly suitable, to-the-point solos. On his own recordings, he was more expansive, developing his solos over a number of choruses with utmost craft.

The artistry exhibited by Wes was ultimately to lead to the redefinition of jazz guitar. His influence has, and continues to reach the oncoming generations of guitarists within, and outside the jazz world. Being on the faculty of Berklee College of Music for several years, I have seen first hand how the music of Wes Montgomery continues to inspire guitarists in pursuit of excellence. Even those not versed in jazz get excited about Wes' playing because it simply feels so good.

When working with these transcriptions, keep the recordings close at hand and refer to them continually. What can be communicated on the printed page is limited, but your listening to the recordings will help to make the written notes come to life.

A word about the tablature fingerings. When deciding fingerings I considered the following factors:

1. Playability - Where does the particular phrase lie well on the fingerboard?
2. Harmonic relation - What chord shape or shapes does this phrase imply?
3. Timbre - Does the timbre clearly indicate which string a note was played on?

I have not presumed, nor do I intend to imply, where every note was originally played by these fingerings. My intention is to provide fingerings that work well with this music. Due to the nature of the guitar, I also recommend practicing phrases in at least one other area of the fingerboard.

Here is a brief summary of the transcribed music.

Wes Montgomery - guitar
All tracks

Scrambled Eggs

Nat Adderly - *cornet* (leader)
Sam Jones - *bass*
Bobby Timmons - *piano*
Louis Hayes - *drums*
recorded January 27, 1960

Scrambled Eggs is from Nat Adderley's highly successful *Work Song* album. The Bobby Timmons composition is a bass feature for Sam Jones who solos during the head breaks. I have included these bass breaks in the transcription as a matter of interest. For the **Scrambled Eggs** melody, Wes plays octave unison with the cornet. Taking the last solo for one chorus, Wes appears to be drawing from the melody by using a great deal of chromaticism in his solo lines. This technique, that is associated with the bebop jazz style, is characterized by the resolution of single or double chromatics to chord tones from above and/or below.

Compulsion

Joe Gordon - *trumpet*
Harold Land - *tenor sax* (leader)
Barry Harris - *piano*
Sam Jones - *bass*
Louis Hayes - *drums*
recorded May 17, 1960

From Harold Land's *West Coast Blues* LP, **Compulsion** begins with trademark octaves from Wes. On the head and solos of his band mates, Wes shares comping duties with Barry Harris. The A section of **Compulsion** has a Im to IVm chord change that leads to descending lydian chord structures. Wes takes the second solo and on his two choruses, skillfully plays through the most active harmonic segments, melodically weaving through the changes. On the lydian segments, Wes transposes short musical fragments in parallel motion with the chord structures. His use of thirds on the final bridge should also be noted.

Terrain

Joe Gordon - *trumpet*
Harold Land - *tenor sax* (leader)
Barry Harris - *piano*
Sam Jones - *bass*
Louis Hayes - *drums*
recorded May 17, 1960

Another tune from Harold Land's *West Coast Blues* album, **Terrain** has Wes comping supportively for Land and Joe Gordon, who play the melody. The multitonal A section chord changes are simplified to a minor key vamp (Im / IIm7b5 / V7b9) for solos. Wes takes the fourth solo.

Ursula

Joe Gordon - *trumpet*
Harold Land - *tenor sax* (leader)
Barry Harris - *piano*
Sam Jones - *bass*
Louis Hayes - *drums*
recorded May 17, 1960

Ursula has Wes again with the Harold Land group playing the melody with Land and Gordon. I have included Land's sax breaks in the transcription. This Harold Land composition has an A section with an 11 measure phrase length, including a bar of 2/4. Wes starts his solo at the bridge changes after Gordon's, playing bright upper structure tensions over the II-V progressions. The bittersweet quality of this Land composition is reflected throughout Wes' solo as he defies the harmonic complexity with plaintively melodic lines.

Lolita

Julian "Cannonball" Adderly - *alto sax* (leader)
Victor Feldman - *vibes*
Ray Brown - *bass*
Louis Hayes - *drums*
recorded May 21, 1960

Lolita was originally released on the *Cannonball Adderly And The Poll Winner* LP on Riverside. The Latin styled head serves as a platform for launching into swing solos. Under the melody of **Lolita**, Wes comps concerted rhythms with Cannonball and outlines the minor "line cliches" through the chord changes. The third solo is Wes' and he plays with a sense of time that's truly incomparable. His eighth notes seem to find their "pocket" resulting in a glorious swing feel. On the sequence of II / V / I progressions, Wes arpeggiates triplets through chordal upper structures that yield colorful tensions and extended chord tones. For the entire second chorus, Wes employs his characteristic octave technique with astounding facility and musicality.

Tune Up

James Clay - *flute*
Victor Feldman - *piano*
Sam Jones - *bass*
Louis Hayes - *drums*
recorded October 12, 1960

From the Wes Montgomery *Movin' Along* album, **Tune Up** is probably the most unusual recording in this collection. Wes used a 6 string Danelectro bass guitar for contrast against James Clay's flute, as a saxophonist may opt for a baritone over a tenor sax, flugel horn for trumpet, etc. The notation is written so that notes will sound an octave higher when played on a standard guitar. Regardless of the register, **Tune Up** is a vital addition to this set. Wes solos for six choruses, taking each one to greater heights. Note that for the solos, an auxiliary IIm7 / V7 change is added up a half step, one measure before the Dm7 and Cm7 chord changes as an extra hurdle.

Says You

James Clay - *flute*
Victor Feldman - *piano*
Sam Jones - *bass*
Louis Hayes - *drums*
recorded October 12, 1960

Says You, a Sam Jones composition, was originally released on the Wes Montgomery *Movin' Along* album. Wes intersperses octaves with single notes on the melody, played with Victor Feldman on piano. Note the development of his three chorus solo. On the first chorus, Wes plays roughly four bar mid register phrases, never going higher than the 1st string C. At the second chorus, longer phrases are introduced and the overall range increases. His third time through the chord changes, the harmonic content and range of the solo line again expand. Wes peaks on the last bridge with sequences, triplets through chordal upper structures and multi-octave arpeggios. The solo is capped off with eight bars of Wes digging into the blues, working off C major and minor blues scales.

Delirium

The Montgomery Brothers
Buddy Montgomery - piano
Monk Montgomery - bass
Bobby Thomas - drums
recorded January 3, 1961

Wes used block chords and octaves for the melody of **Delirium**, a Harold Land composition from the Montgomery Brothers' *Groove Yard* LP. Jazz guitar great Pat Martino reveals in his instructional video that the *Groove Yard* album was very influential in his musical development. Only soloing for one chorus, Wes establishes a linear momentum that Martino often displays. The unrelenting drive combined with the harmonic content and blues elements of this solo add up to an exciting performance from Wes.

No Hard Feelings

Buddy Montgomery - *vibes*
George Shearing - *piano*
Monk Montgomery - *bass*
Walter Perkins - *drums*
recorded October 9, 1961

No Hard Feelings is from the *George Shearing and the Montgomery' Brothers* album. Wes shares the melody with Buddy Montgomery who is on vibes for this highly arranged track. Lying out while Shearing solos on the A sections, Wes begins his solo at the bridge, traversing the shifting tonal centers up to the end of the chorus.

Dan Bowden

Dan Bowden is a guitarist and music educator who resides in Brookline, Ma. with his wife and son. Having graduated from Berklee College of Music in 1980, he joined the Berklee guitar faculty in 1989 where he teaches blues, jazz and rock styles. Dan has, and continues to perform extensively around New England. Other transcription books available by Dan Bowden are: *Mance Lipscomb, Texas Blues Guitar Solos* and *Lightnin' Hopkins, Blues Guitar Legend*. Dan can be contacted via the Internet at dbowden@it.berklee.edu.

Scrambled Eggs

Sam Jones

Medium Fast Bebop

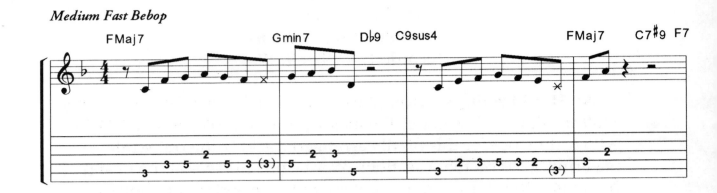

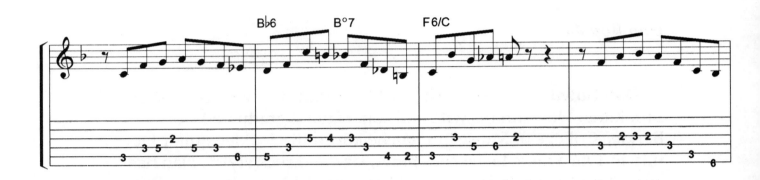

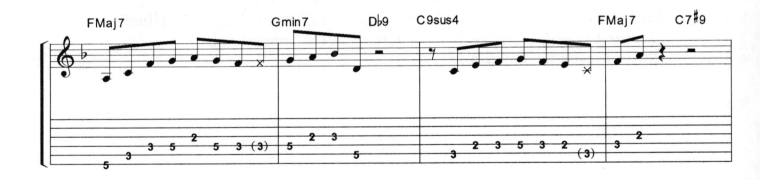

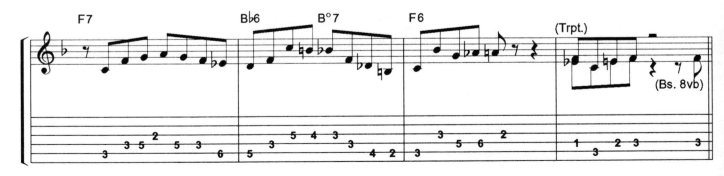

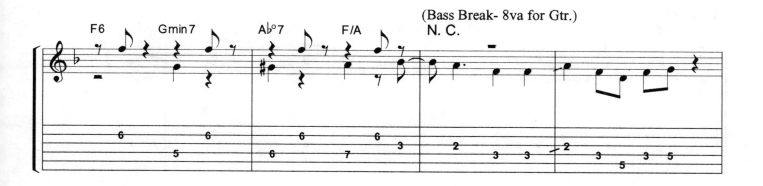

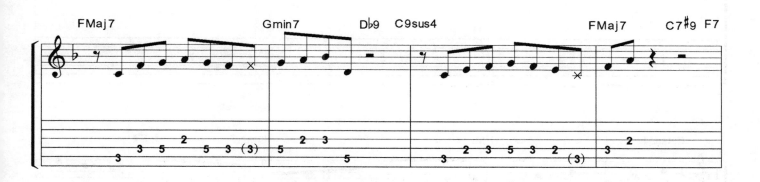

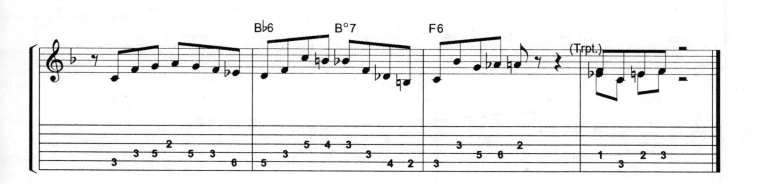

Wes' Solo

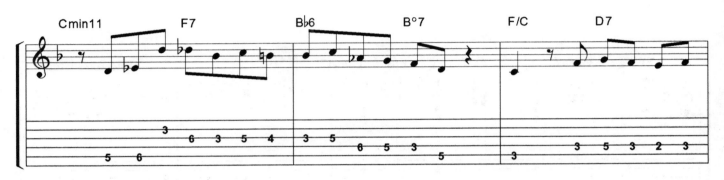

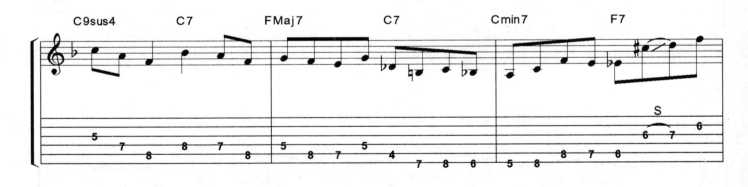

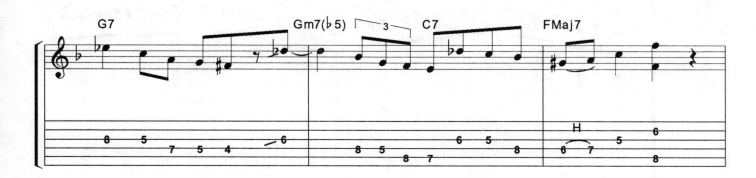
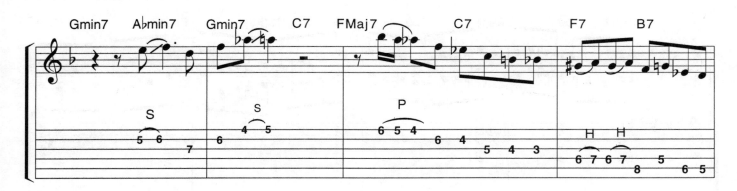

Compulsion

Harold Land

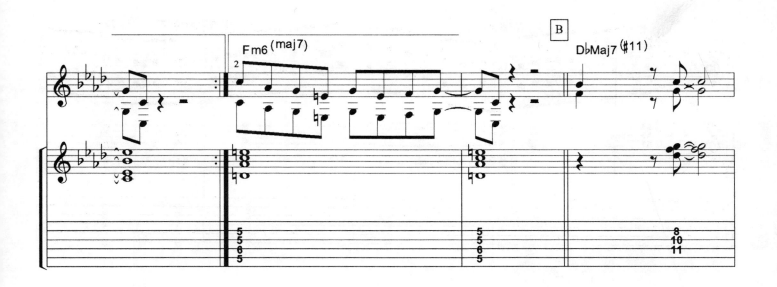

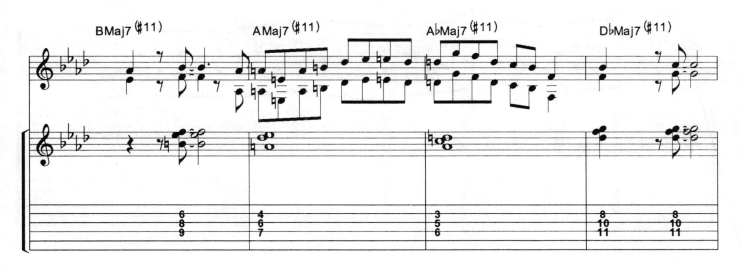

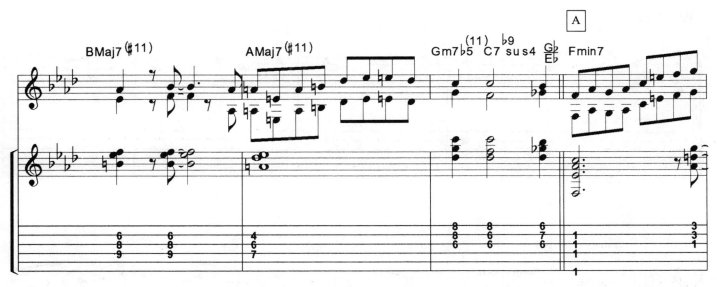

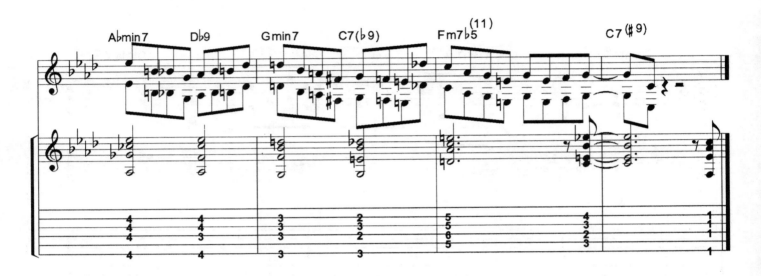

Wes' Solo

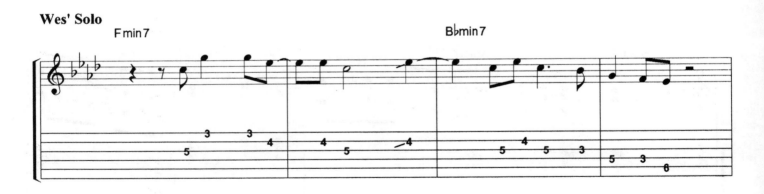

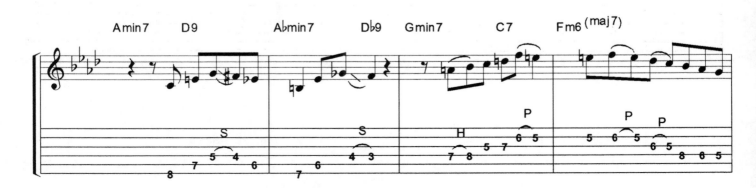

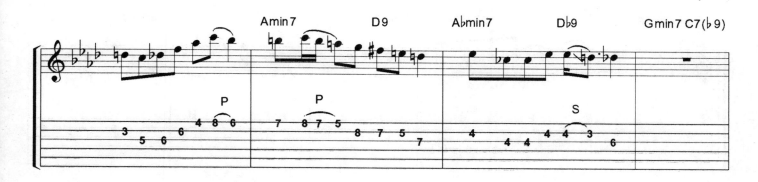

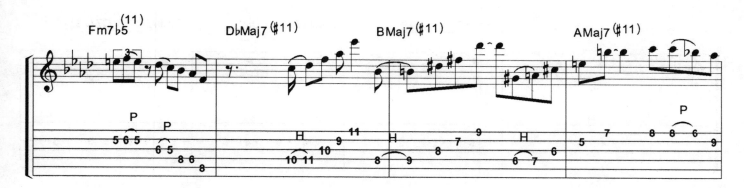

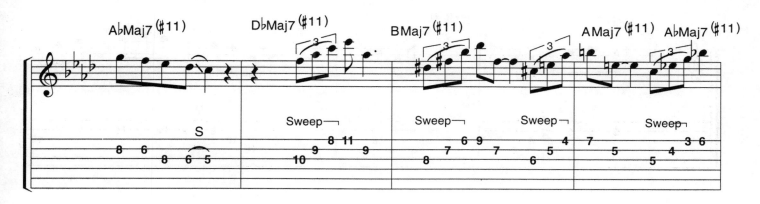

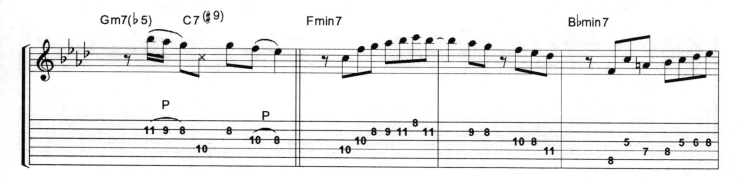

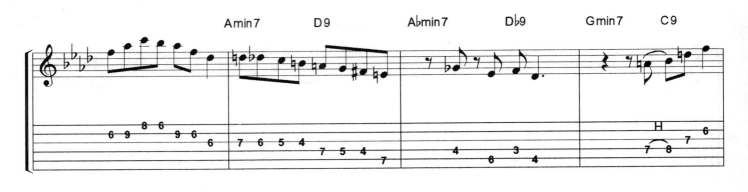

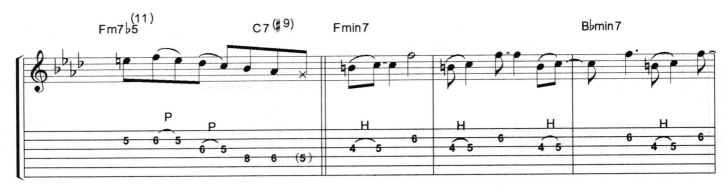

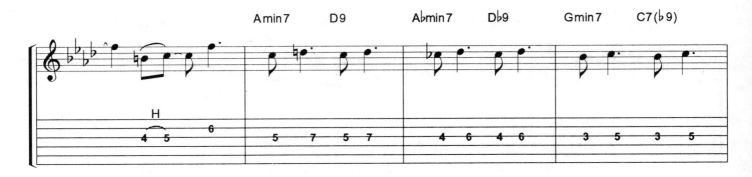

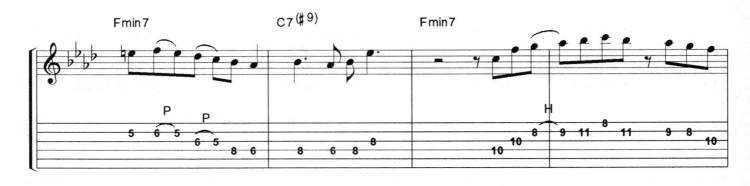

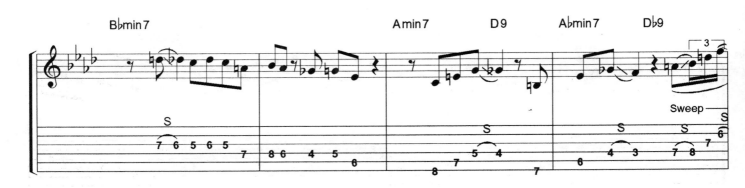

20

Terrain

Harold Land

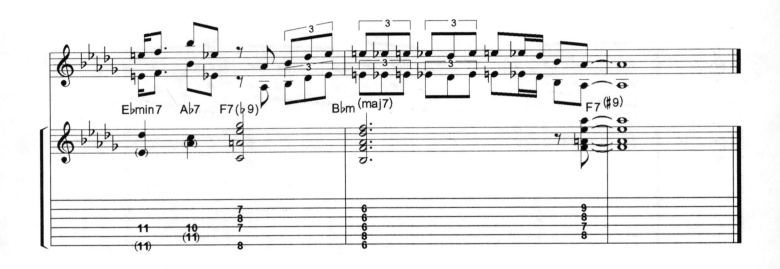

Wes' Solo

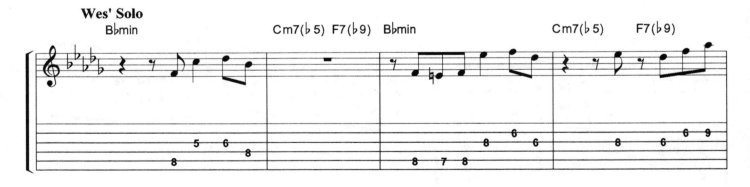

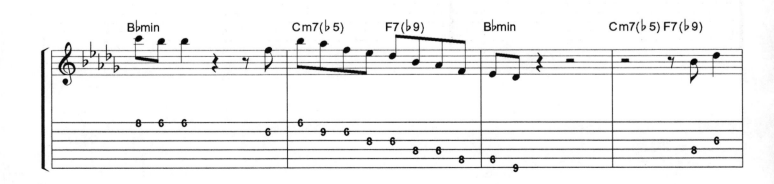

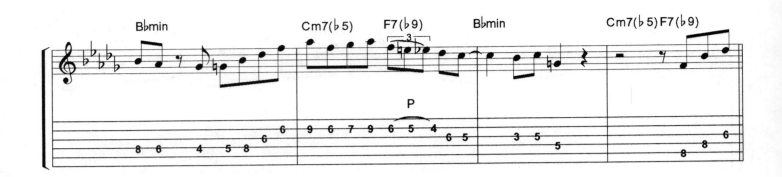

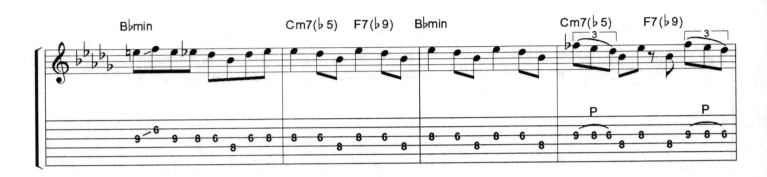

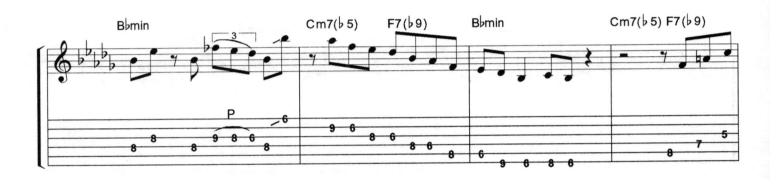

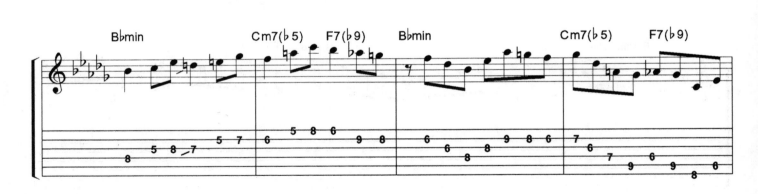

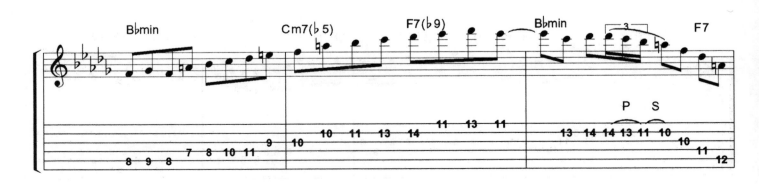

26

Ursula

Harold Land

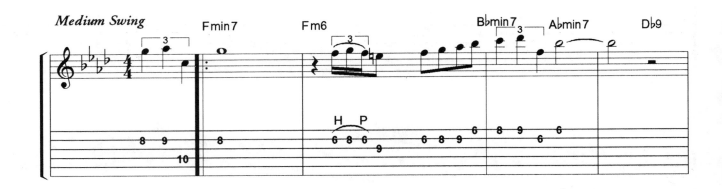

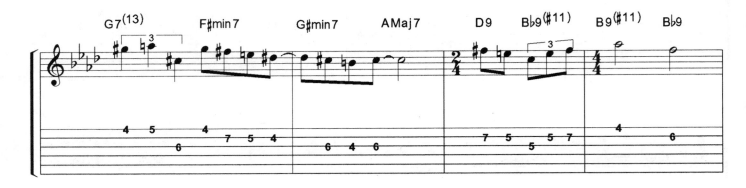

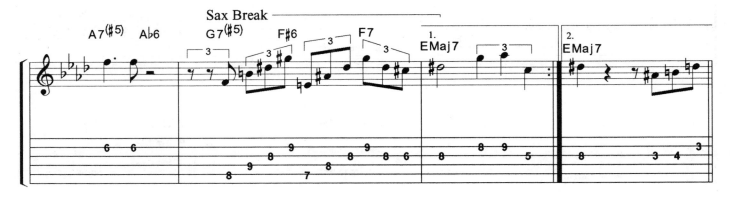

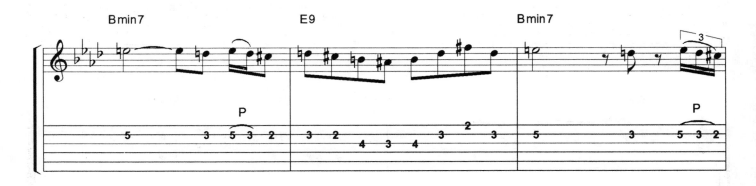

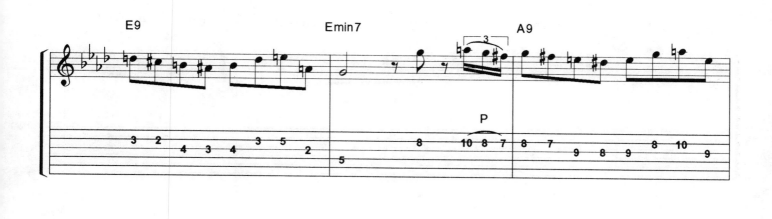

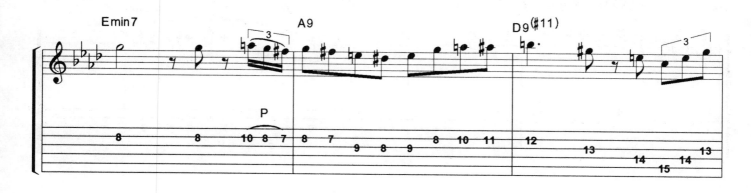

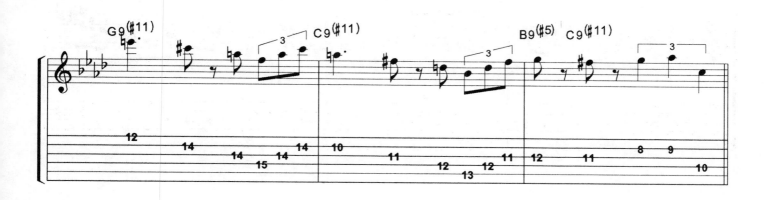

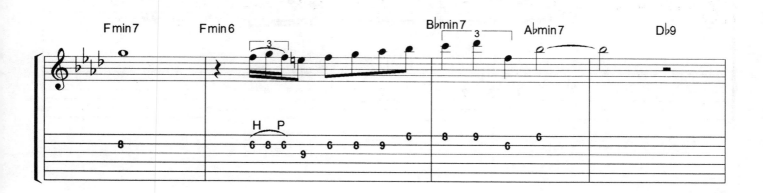

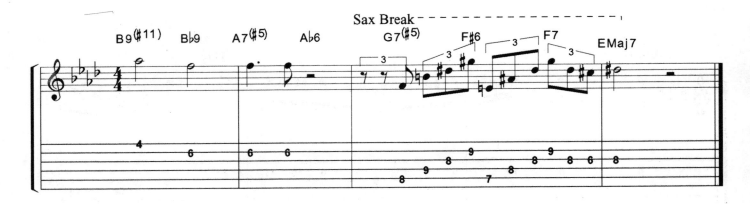

Wes' Solo

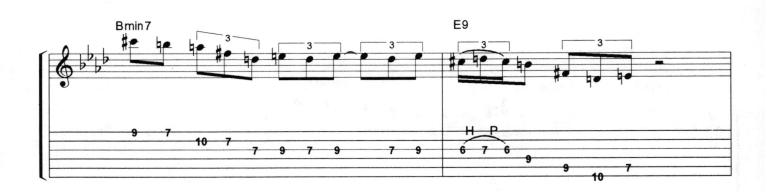

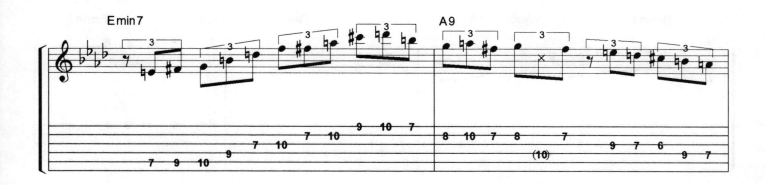

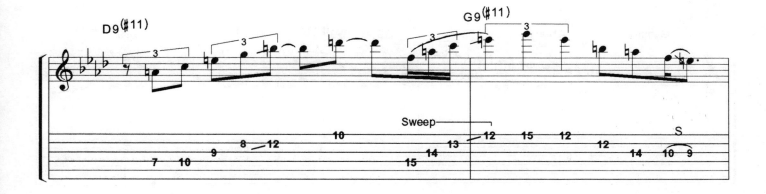

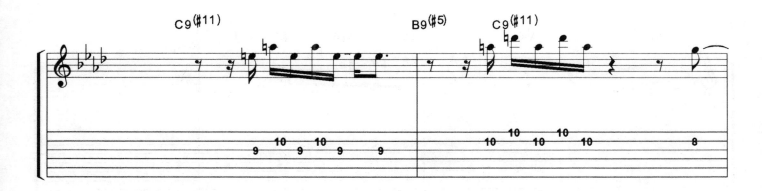

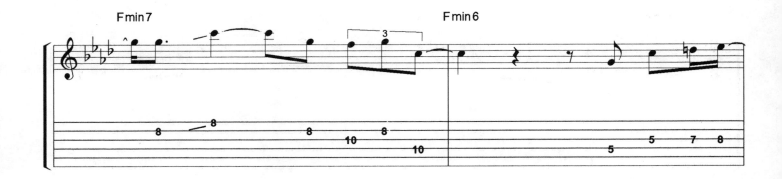

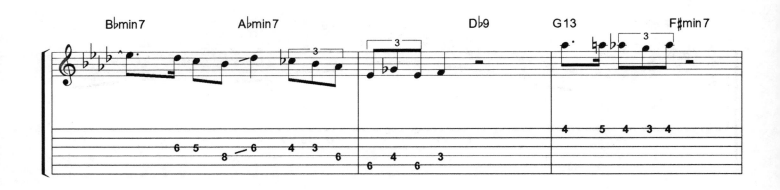

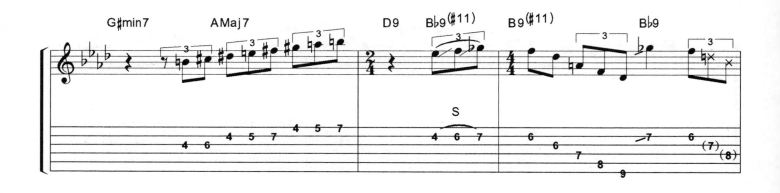

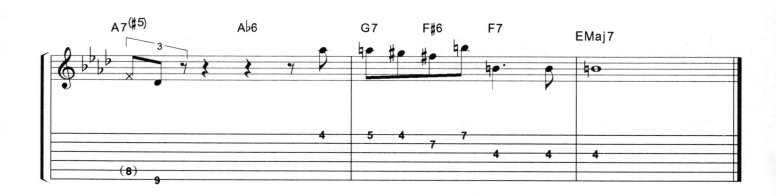

Lolita

Barry Harris

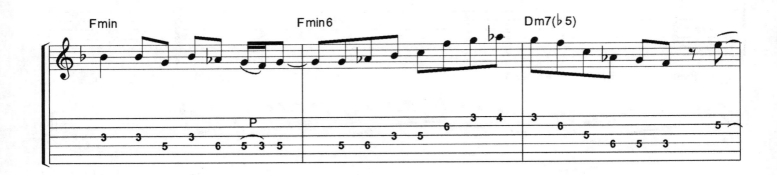

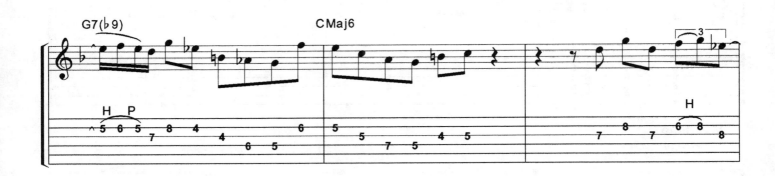

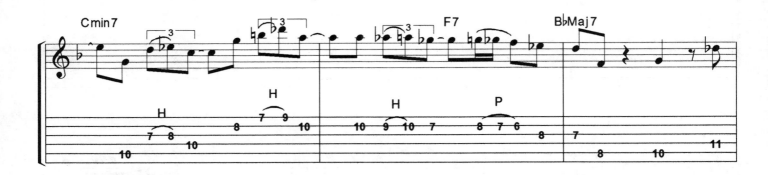

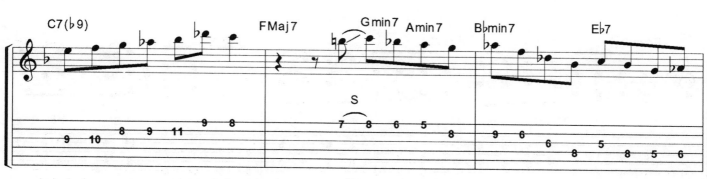

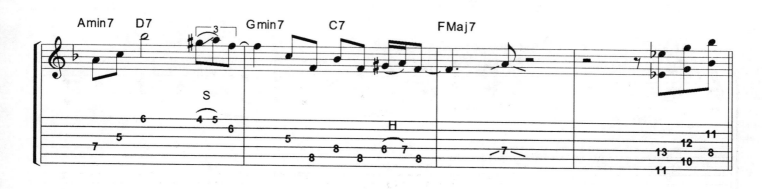

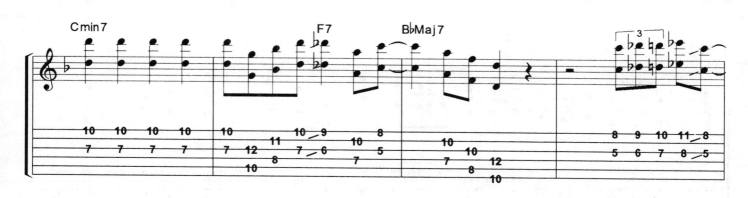

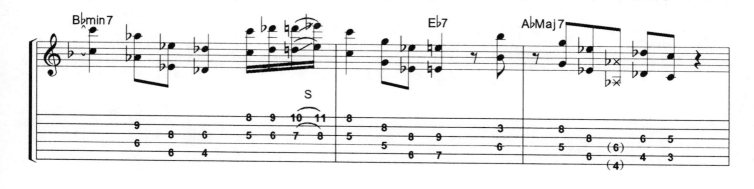

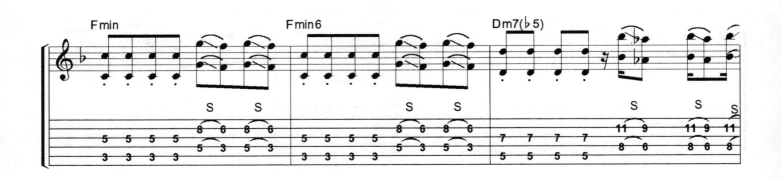

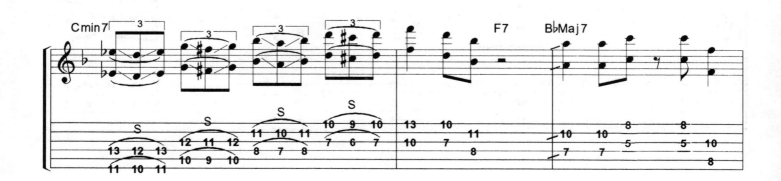

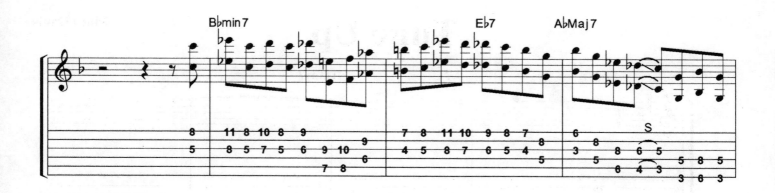

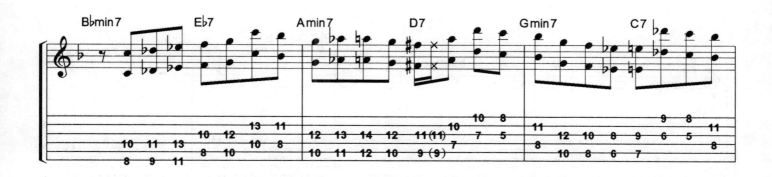

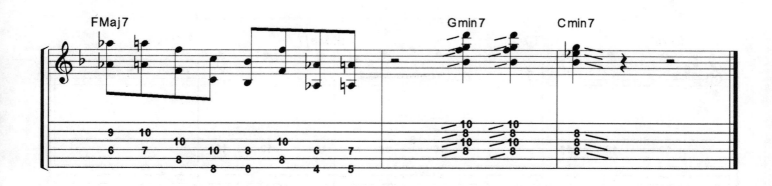

Tune Up

Miles Davis

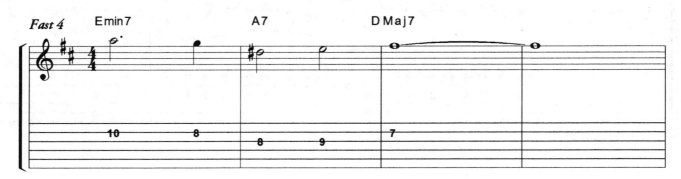

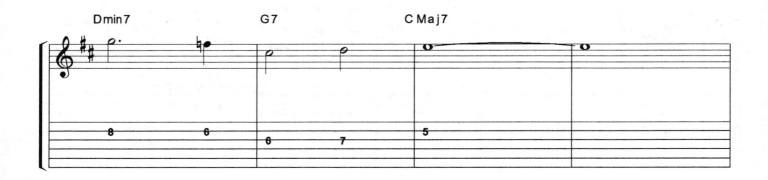

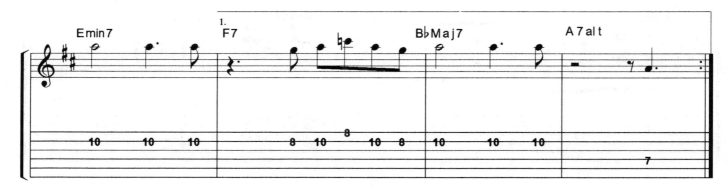

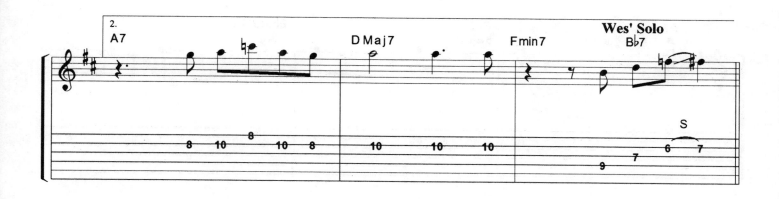

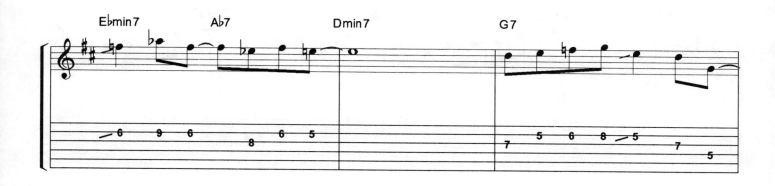

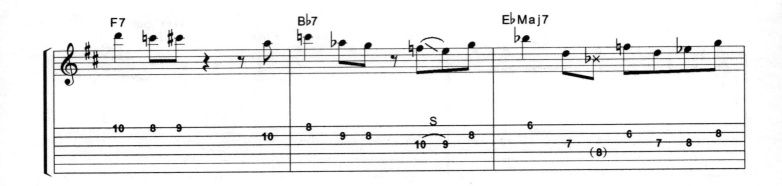

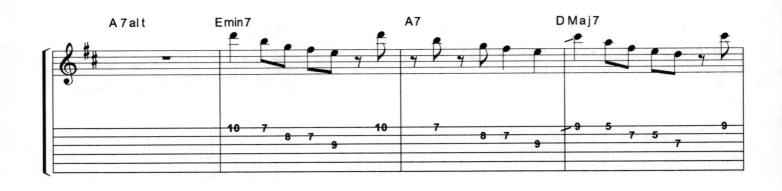

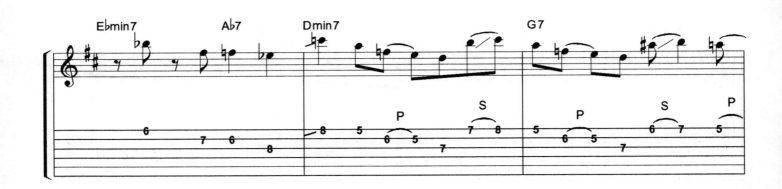

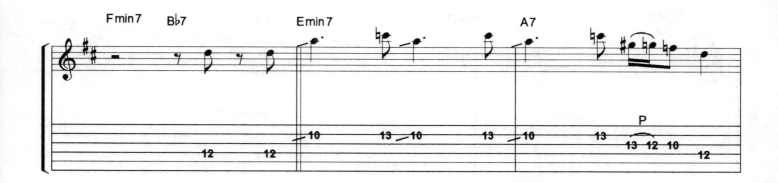

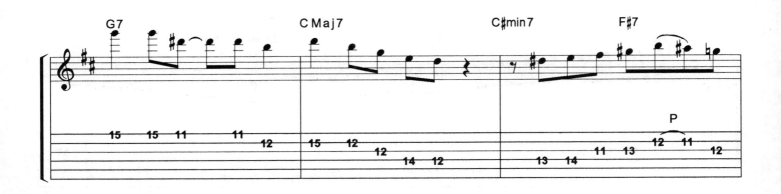

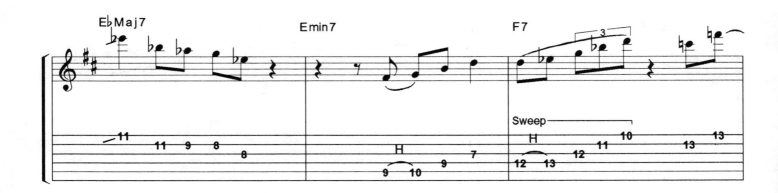

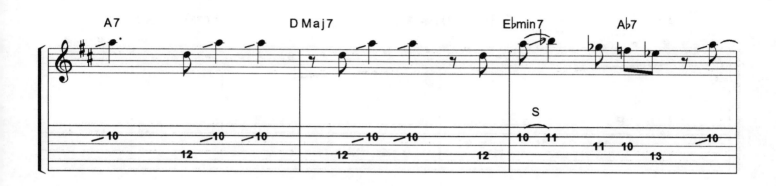

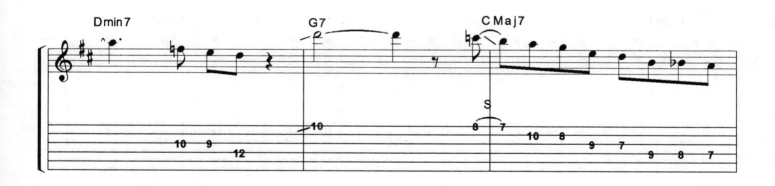

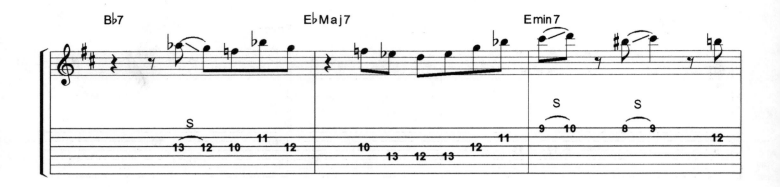

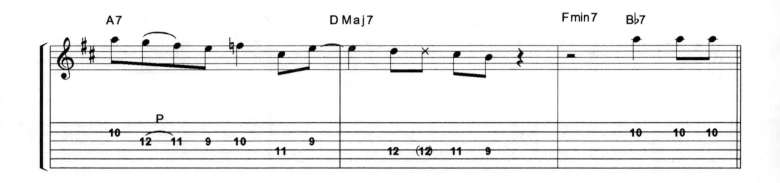

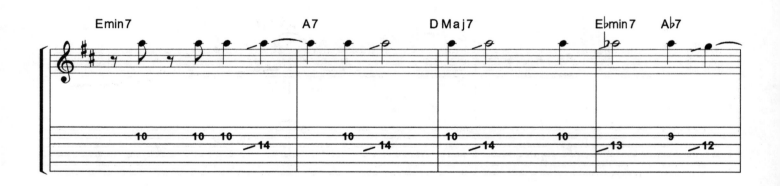

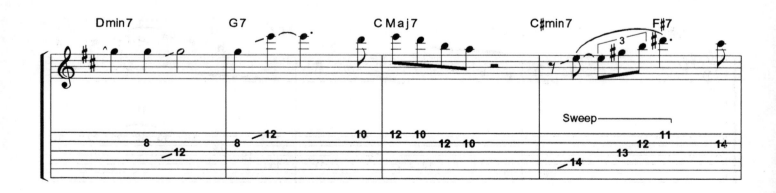

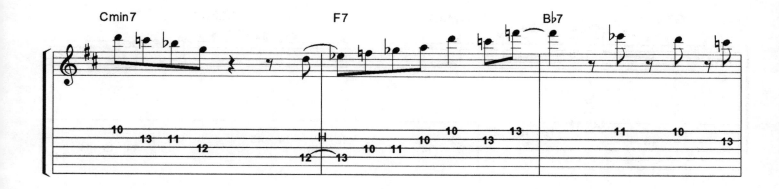

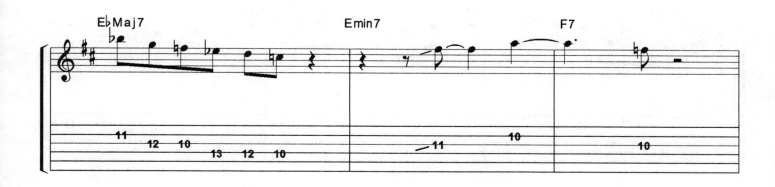

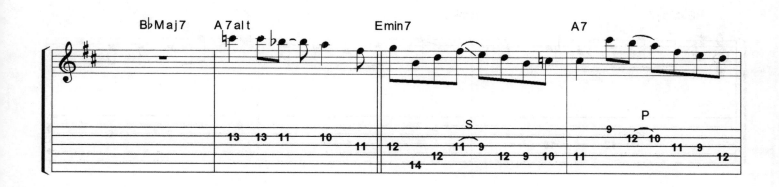

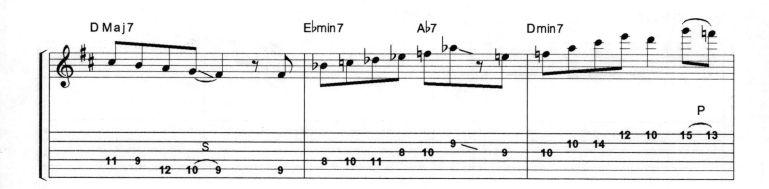

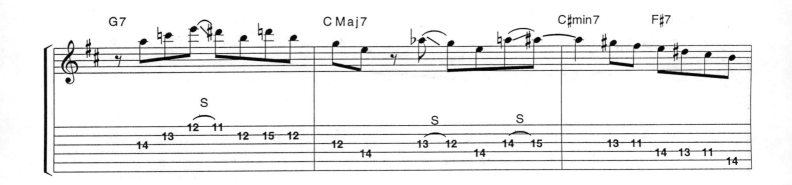

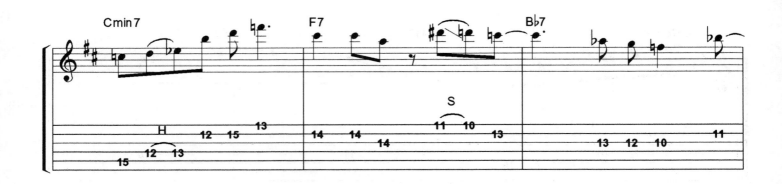

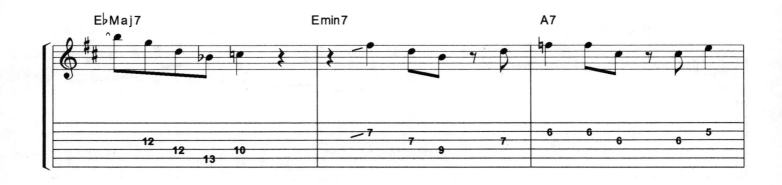

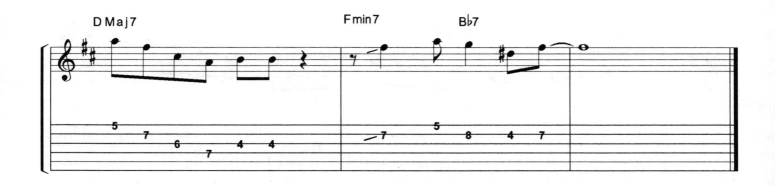

Says You

Sam Jones

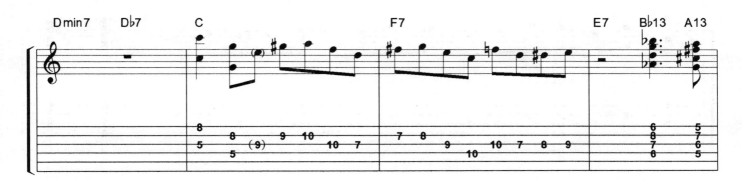

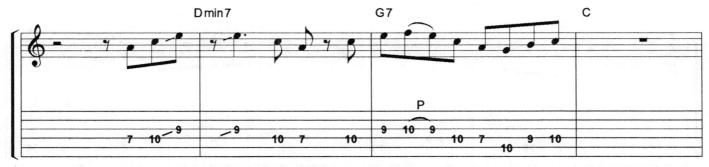

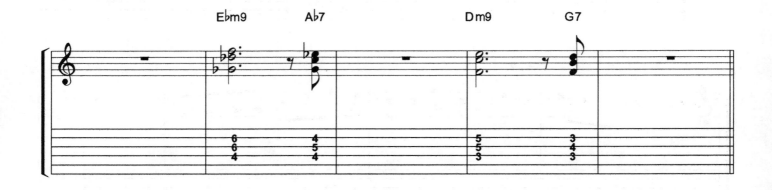

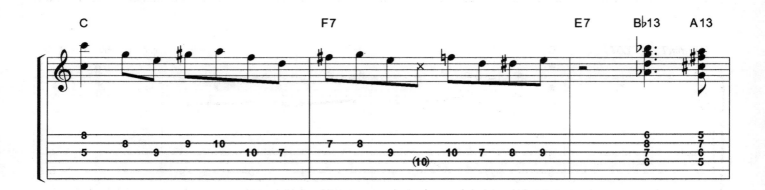

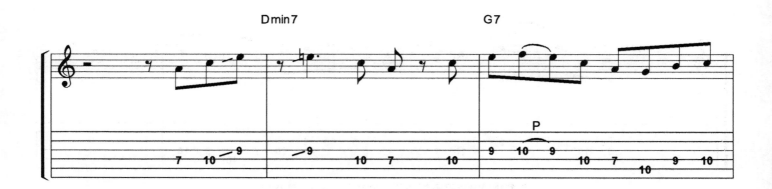

Wes' Solo

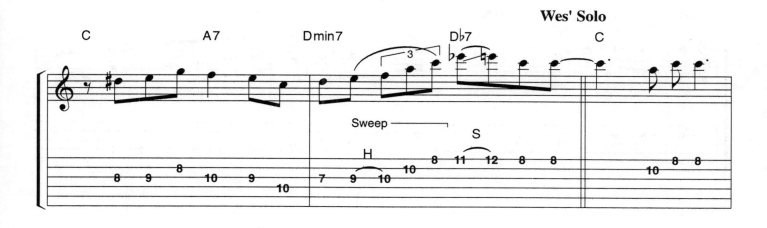

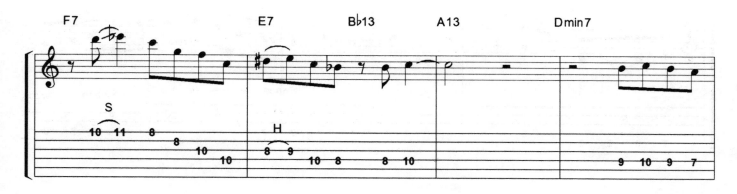

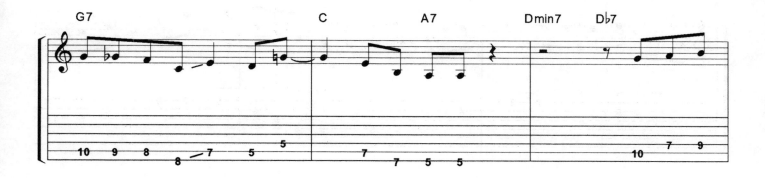

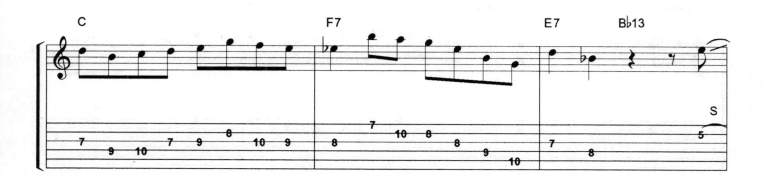

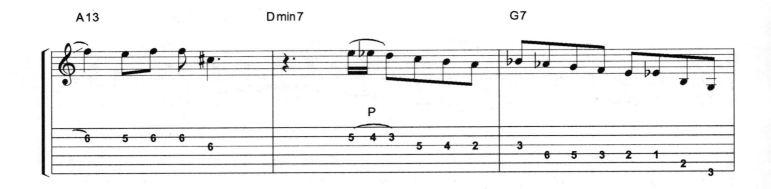

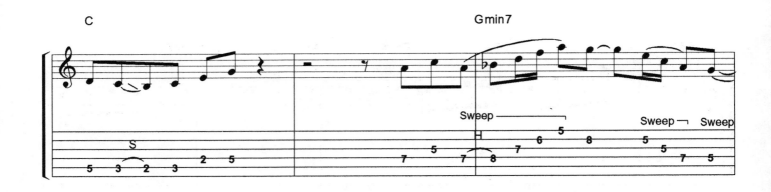

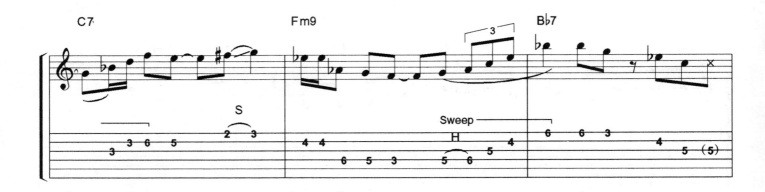

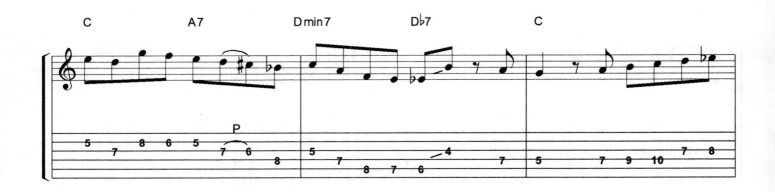

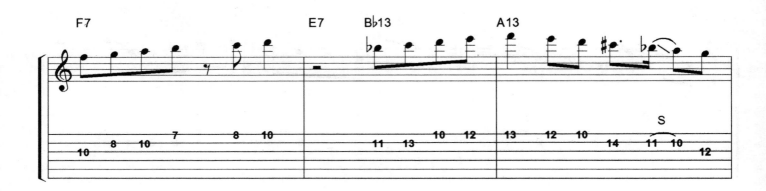

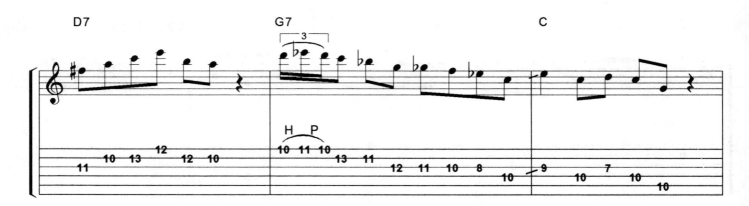

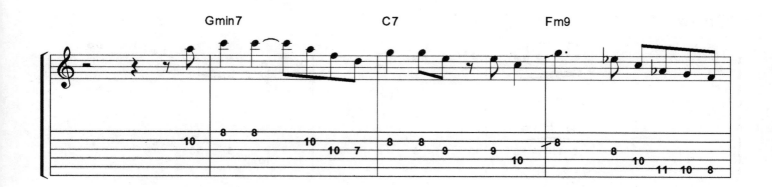

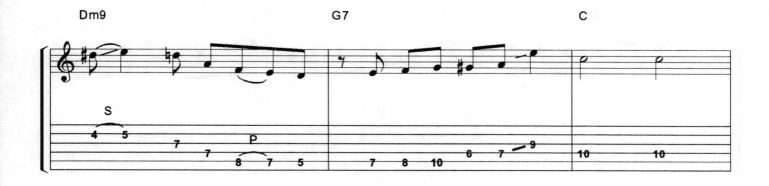

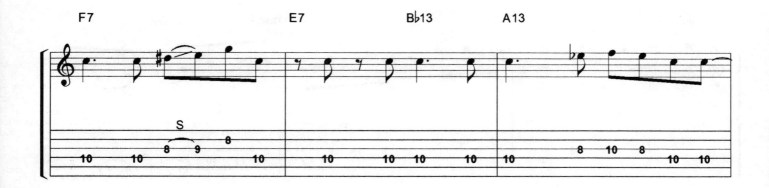

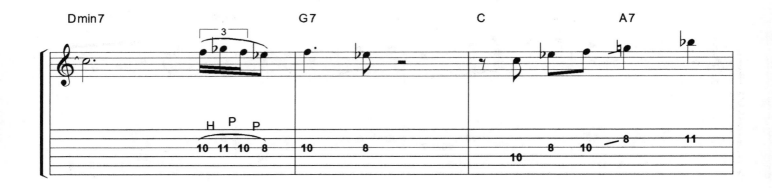

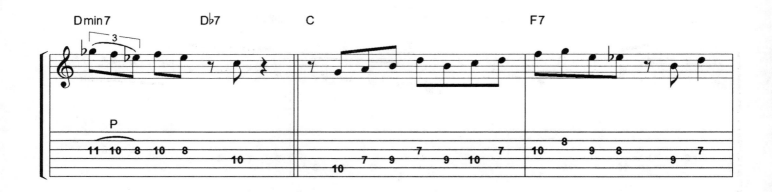

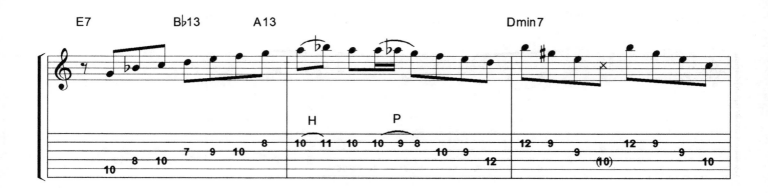

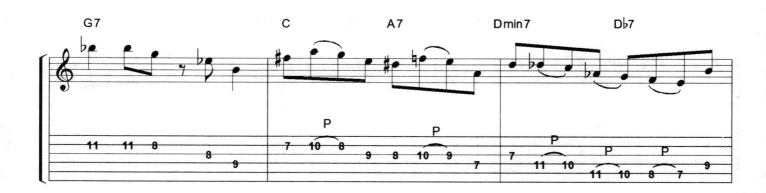

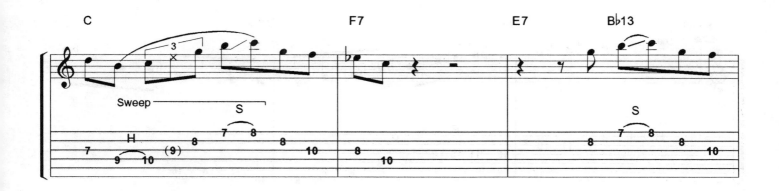

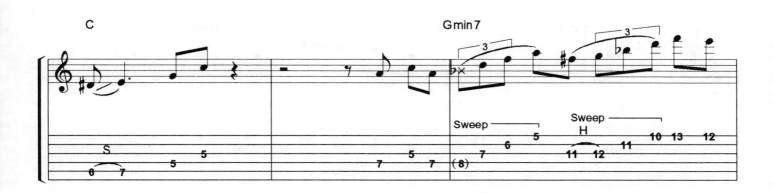

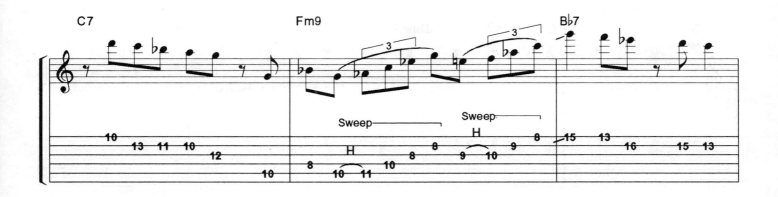

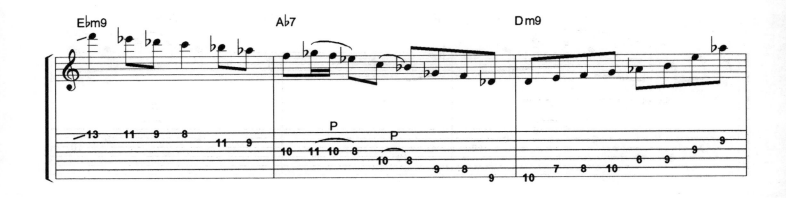

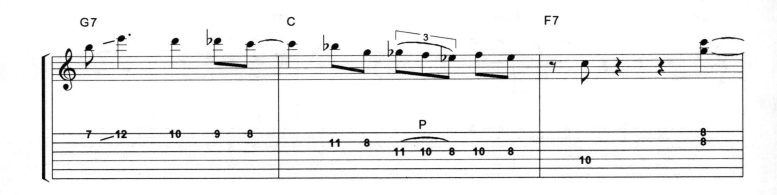

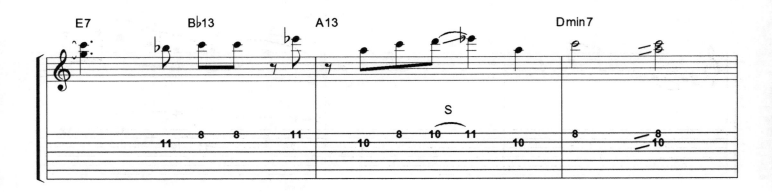

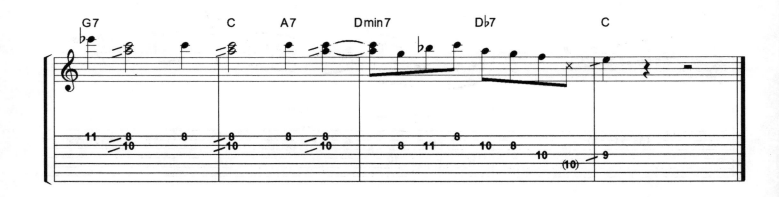

Delirium

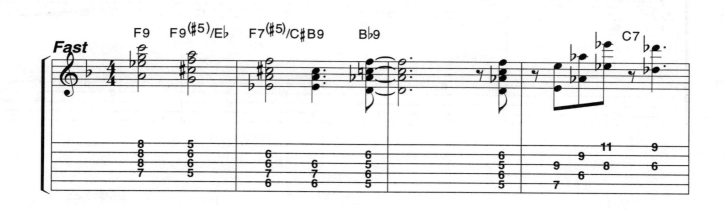

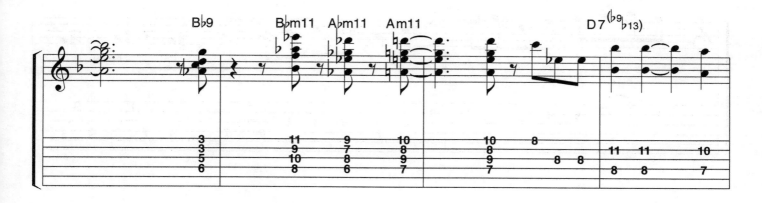

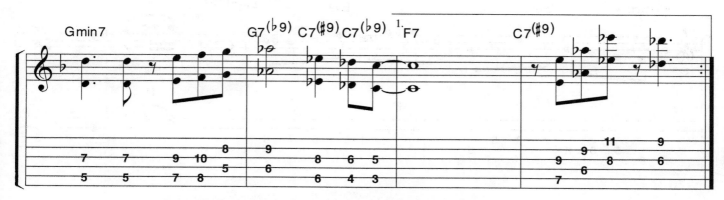

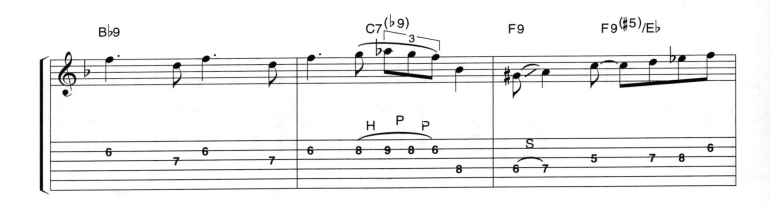

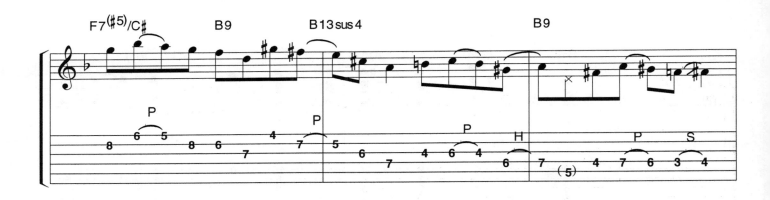

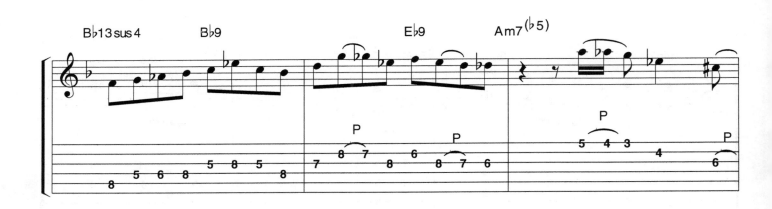

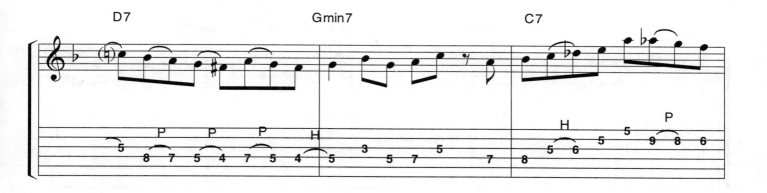

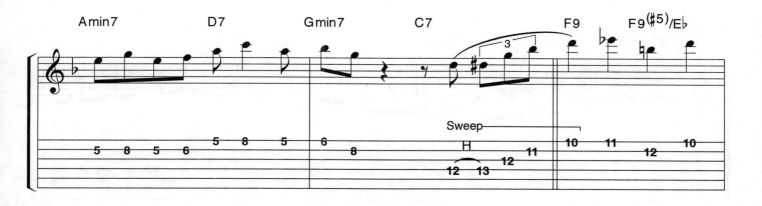

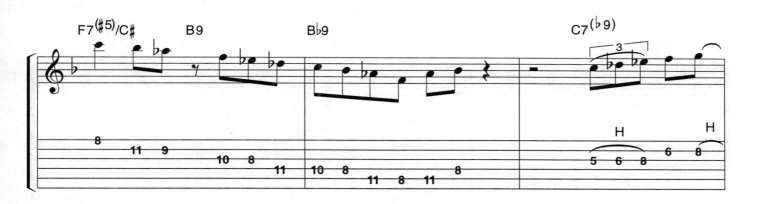

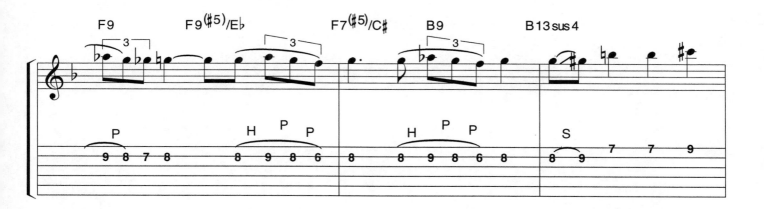

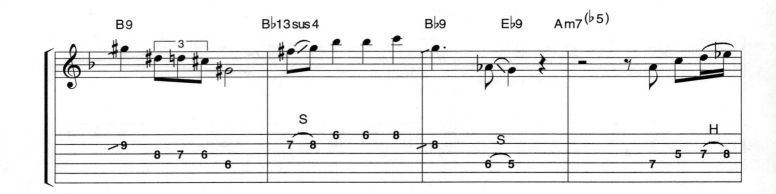

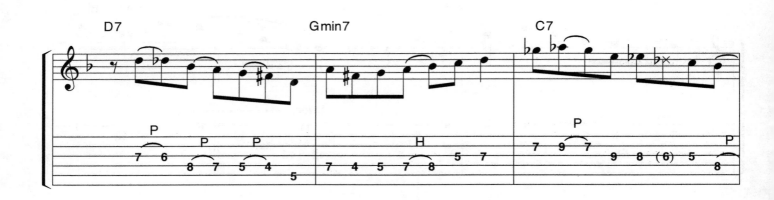

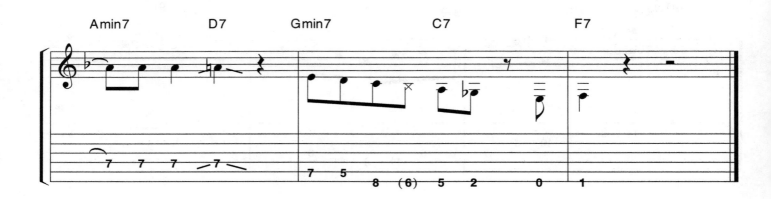

No Hard Feelings

B. Montgomery

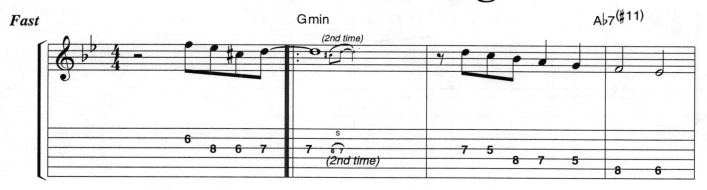

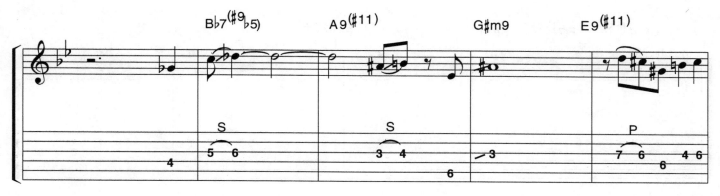

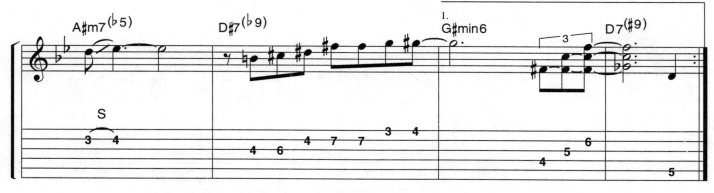

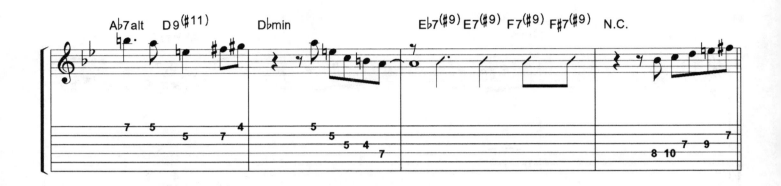

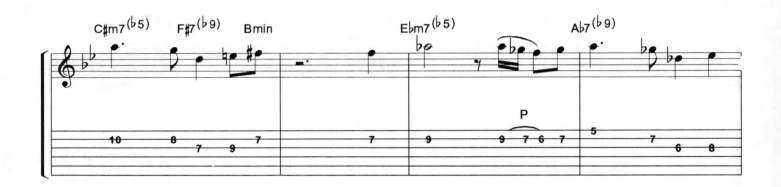

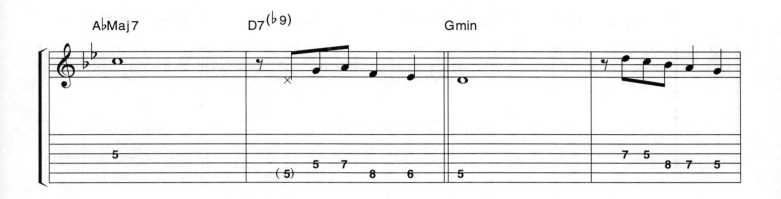

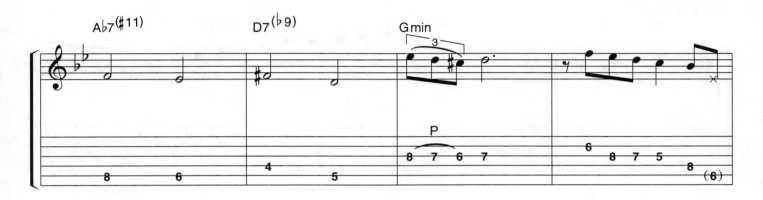

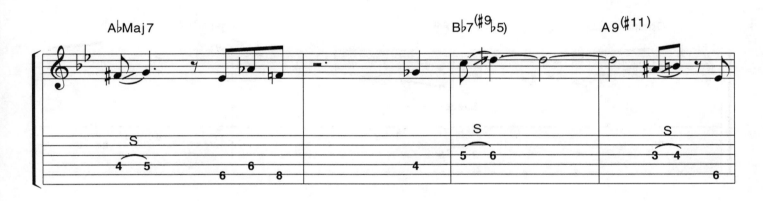

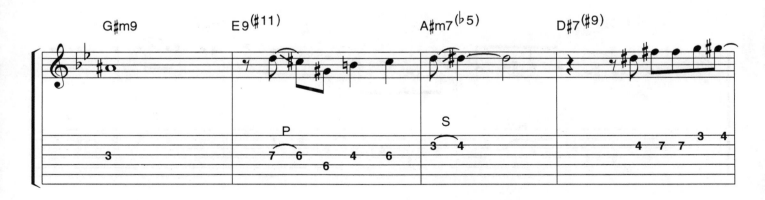

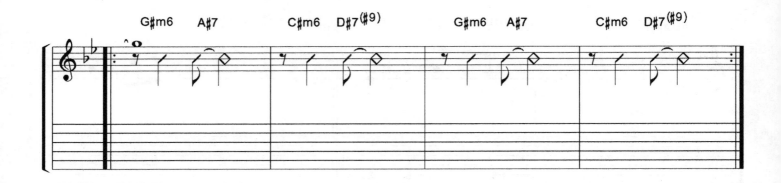

Wes' Solo

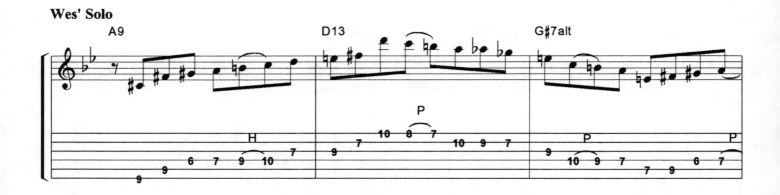

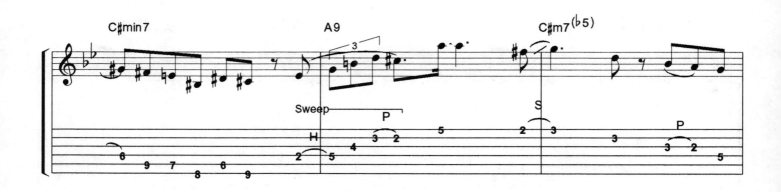

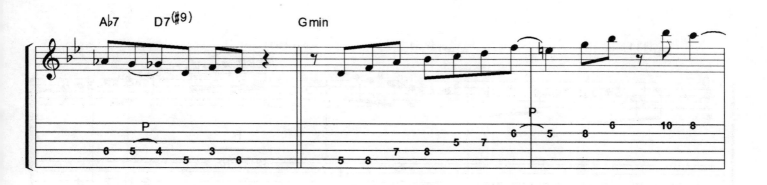

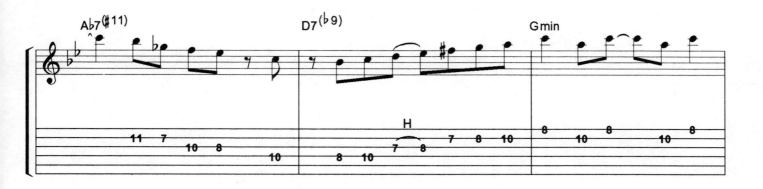

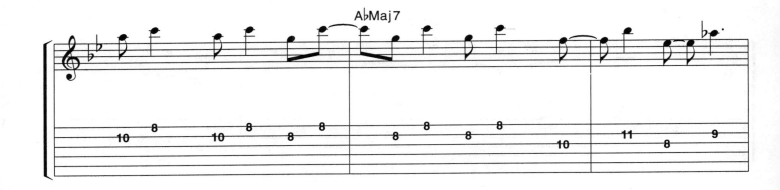

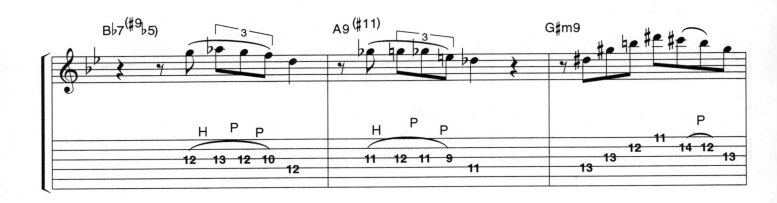

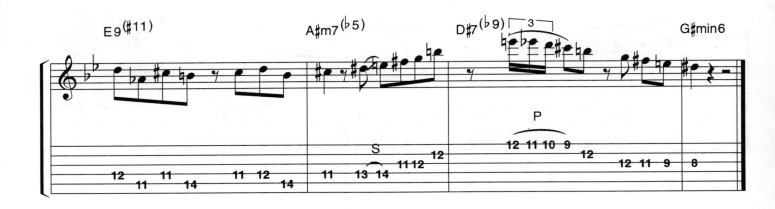